CW00322341

DON'T BE A D*CK

DON'T BE A D*CK

An Hachette UK Company
www.hachette.co.uk

Summersdale Publishers Ltd
Part of Octopus Publishing Group Limited
Carmelite House
50 Victoria Embankment
LONDON
EC4Y 0DZ
UK

www.summersdale.com

Printed and bound in China

ISBN: 978-1-78783-286-2

Substantial discounts on bulk quantities of Summersdale books are available to corporations, professional associations and other organizations. For details contact general enquiries: telephone: +44 (0) 1243 771107 or email: enquiries@summersdale.com.

DON'T BE A

D*CK

JOSEPH DEWEY

summersdale

LADIES, GENTLEMEN AND EVERYONE IN-BETWEEN, THIS IS A NEW TYPE OF SELF-HELP BOOK THAT WILL GIVE YOU A SLAP AROUND THE FACE AND ONE HELL OF A WAKE-UP CALL. I PROMISE YOU WILL FIND THIS TO BE A HELPFUL, HILARIOUS HANDBOOK.

IT MAY BE A LITTLE BIT RUDE, BUT IT WILL OFFER YOU SIMPLE INSTRUCTIONS ON HOW NOT TO BE A **D*CK** IN LIFE, BECAUSE LET'S FACE IT, THERE ARE ENOUGH OF THEM AROUND.

DON'T
PUNCH
PEOPLE

PICK YOUR BATTLES WISELY

DON'T LOSE YOUR SH*T

WAIT FOR THE GREEN LIGHT

GRAB LIFE BY THE BALLS

DON'T BE
SEXIST

DON'T BE OFFENDED WHEN PEOPLE THINK YOU ARE BEING SEXIST

CLEAN UP AFTER YOURSELF

STOP LEAVING DIRTY DISHES IN THE SINK

SMILE MORE

VISIT THE DENTIST

BRUSH
YOUR TEETH

TELL YOUR FRIEND IF THERE IS SOMETHING IN THEIR TEETH

DON'T LICK PEOPLE'S FACES

BUY YOUR
ROUND

BE A FUN DRUNK

LOOK IN THE EYE WHEN YOU CHEERS

DRINK
RESPONSIBLY

DON'T BE OFFENDED IF YOUR FRIEND HAS A SOFT DRINK

CLOWN
AROUND
HARMLESSLY

DON'T PICK YOUR NOSE

DON'T EAT THAT BOGEY

DON'T FLICK THAT BOGEY

SNEEZE INTO A F*CKING TISSUE

COVER YOUR MOUTH WHEN YOU COUGH

WASH
YOUR HANDS

CHECK
YOUR FLY

DON'T **PEE**
ON THE
TOILET SEAT

PUT THE F*CKING TOILET SEAT BACK DOWN

NO

MEANS NO

DON'T BE
CREEPY

DON'T BE A PERV

DON'T EXPOSE YOURSELF

PLEASE THE
OTHER LOVER
FIRST

KISS WITH YOUR EYES SHUT

LOVE PASSIONATELY

F*CK HARD

USE A
CONDOM

TELL PEOPLE IF YOU HAVE AN STI

CLEAN
UNDER YOUR
GENITALS

DON'T HAVE SMELLY GENITALS

DON'T HAVE SMELLY FEET

DON'T OVERSHARE

DON'T BE A
F*CKBOY

TEXT BACK

ASK
QUESTIONS

DON'T GIVE
MIXED
SIGNALS

DON'T BE
A KISS-ASS

DON'T BE HOMOPHOBIC

DON'T BE A
BIGOT

DON'T BE RACIST

SAY PLEASE
AND
THANK YOU

DON'T BE OFFENDED BY SATIRE

CALM THE F*CK DOWN

DON'T CLIP YOUR TOENAILS IN PUBLIC

BE CLASSY

STAY COOL

GET YOUR HANDS OUT OF YOUR **PANTS**

DON'T BE A JERK

PULL YOUR
TROUSERS UP

TAKE YOUR HOOD DOWN INDOORS

CUT THE LABEL OFF YOUR CLOTHES

DON'T JUDGE
PEOPLE BY
WHAT THEY'RE
WEARING

DRESS FOR YOURSELF

BE BEAUTIFUL ON THE INSIDE

BE SMART

DON'T TAKE AGES AT THE ATM

VISIT YOUR GRANDPARENTS

DRINK
COFFEE

DON'T DRINK
TOO MUCH
COFFEE

DON'T DRINK
SH*T COFFEE

DON'T PUT THE MILK IN FIRST

TAKE A
CHILL PILL

CHILL THE F*CK OUT

DON'T
TAKE DRUGS

HAVE A
LAUGH

STOP
F*CKING
ABOUT

DON'T BE A
PR*CK

BE LESS
OF A C*NT

SWEAR LESS

APOLOGIZE WHEN NECESSARY

HOLD THAT FART IN

OWN UP TO THE BAD FART SMELL

KNOW WHEN TO USE AIR FRESHENER

THE QUIET CARRIAGE MEANS SHUT THE F*CK UP

DON'T PLAY LOUD MUSIC ON PUBLIC TRANSPORT

ENJOY
GOOD MUSIC

RESPECT

LISTEN TO
PODCASTS

BE READY
AT AIRPORT
SECURITY

MANAGE YOUR TIME EFFECTIVELY

OFFER
THAT SEAT

LET OTHERS **MERGE** INTO YOUR LANE

BE A
GOOD
FRIEND

TAKE CHARGE OF YOUR DESTINY

TAKE
REJECTION
ON THE CHIN

DON'T ACT ENTITLED, YOU ARE OWED NOTHING

PAY YOUR PARENTS BACK

STOP
B*TCHING

DON'T BE
A BULLY

DON'T PUSH PEOPLE'S BUTTONS

DON'T
PUSH
PEOPLE

DON'T BE A PUSHOVER

BE MORE
POSITIVE

GIVE UP
THE WORD
"SHOULDN'T"

GIVE UP THE WORD "CAN'T"

DON'T BE AFRAID TO SAY YES

DON'T BE AFRAID TO SAY NO

STOP
PROCRASTINATING

STOP CLICKING THAT PEN

GIVE THE F*CKING PEN BACK AFTER YOU USE IT

DON'T STEAL THINGS

CUT THE
BULLSH*T

DON'T TROLL PEOPLE

ACCEPT THAT OTHER PEOPLE MAY HAVE A DIFFERENT OPINION THAN YOU

UNDERSTAND WHAT YOU HAVE DONE WRONG

THINK
BEFORE
YOU TWEET

BE
INTERESTING

SUPPORT YOUR FRIENDS' VENTURES AND SUCCESSES

BANTER BUT DON'T BE RUDE

DON'T BE
COCKY

ENJOY
SARCASM

GROW A
THICK SKIN

DON'T SWEAT THE SMALL STUFF

DON'T HOG THE CHARGER

DON'T SMACK YOUR LIPS

DON'T SNORE

SHARE THE F*CKING BLANKETS

KNOW WHEN TO SHUT THE F*CK UP

KNOW WHEN TO SPEAK UP

KNOW YOUR VALUES

TRUST
YOUR GUT

GIVE PRAISE

WHERE

IT'S DUE

BE A
SHOULDER
TO CRY ON

DON'T BE AFRAID TO CRY

STOP
STARING

GO AND
SAY HELLO

KNOW WHEN TO LEAVE PEOPLE ALONE

GO TO PRIDE

BE AN ALLY

MARCH FOR
EQUALITY

PICK UP
YOUR
RUBBISH

RECYCLE YOUR WASTE

USE A REUSABLE CUP

SAY NO TO THAT F*CKING PLASTIC STRAW

VOLUNTEER MORE

ENJOY
NATURE

SUPPORT
A CHARITY

PROTECT
THIS PLANET

LET THE PAST
BE THE PAST

LEAVE
YOUR ISSUES
AT HOME

ALWAYS PUT IN YOUR BEST EFFORT

STOP MAKING
EXCUSES

SLOW THE
F*CK DOWN

IF YOU ARE HANGRY, EAT

DON'T CHEW LOUDLY

F*CKING
BREATHE
QUIETLY

DON'T
PUT GUM
UNDER
THE TABLE

ONLY EAT
SPICY FOOD
IF YOU CAN
HANDLE
THE HEAT

CHALLENGE YOURSELF

COME OUT OF YOUR COMFORT ZONE

GET OVER YOUR BAD DAY – LIFE IS GOOD

DON'T
GIVE UP

DON'T BE AFRAID OF CHANGE

KEEP IT
REAL

DON'T GET FILLERS –
YOU ARE
BEAUTIFUL
AS YOU ARE

DON'T WEAR TOO MUCH FAKE TAN

WEAR
SUNSCREEN

LIVE LIFE
TO THE FULL

KEEP YOUR HEAD HIGH

TRIM YOUR NOSE HAIR

TRIM
DOWNSTAIRS

STAY TRUE
TO YOURSELF

BELIEVE
IN YOURSELF

KNOW IT WILL ALL BE WORTH IT

ACCEPT THAT SOME PEOPLE ARE JUST C*NTS

ENJOY AND ACCEPT WHERE YOU ARE IN LIFE RIGHT NOW

MAKE A FILM – A PORNO DOESN'T COUNT

MAKE SOME ART – HOWEVER WEIRD IT MAY BE

LEARN TO DANCE – IN F*CKING TIME

SING
MORE – IN
F*CKING
TUNE

WRITE A BOOK – BUT MAKE IT A GOOD BOOK

DON'T JUDGE A BOOK BY ITS COVER

SHARE THAT AMAZING BOOK YOU READ

DON'T BE A D*CK

IF YOU'RE INTERESTED IN FINDING
OUT MORE ABOUT OUR BOOKS, FIND
US ON FACEBOOK AT SUMMERSDALE
PUBLISHERS AND FOLLOW US
ON TWITTER @SUMMERSDALE.

WWW.SUMMERSDALE.COM